# Your Introverted Power

# Your Introverted Power

*An Introverts Guide to Leveraging Your Quiet
Internal Power and Strengths to Succeed in an
Extrovert Dominated World*

Chuck Rikard

Softpress Publishing

SOFTPRESS PUBLISHING
4118 Hickory Crossroads Road
Kenly, NC 27542
softpresspub@gmail.com

**ISBN-10:** 1-5025-4839-9
**ISBN-13:** 978-1-5025-4839-9

**Disclaimer:**
The advice and strategies contained herein may not be suitable for every situation. This work is sold with the understanding that the publisher is not engaged in rendering medical or other professional advice or services. The publisher does not specifically endorse any company or product mentioned or cited in this document. Websites listed were accurate at the time of publishing but may have changed or disappeared between when it was written and when it is read.

No responsibility or liability is assumed by the publisher for any injury, damage or financial loss sustained to persons of property from the use of this information, personal or otherwise, either directly or indirectly. While every effort has been made to ensure reliability and accuracy of the information within, all liability, negligence or otherwise, from any use, misuse or abuse of the operation of any methods, strategies, instructions or ideas contained in the material herein, is sole responsibility of the reader.

All information is generalized, presented for informational purposes only and presented "as is" without warranty or guarantee of any kind.

All trademarks and brands referred to in this book are for illustrative purposes only, are the property of their respective owners and not affiliated with this publication in any way.

# Table of Contents

# Introduction

Do you feel alone in a crowd? Perhaps you prefer a quiet corner to read or contemplate ideas over being in the glare of publicity. Do phones, parties, or work meetings overwhelm you? If this sounds familiar, you are probably an introvert.

What if I told you that introversion has nothing to do with being shy or timid? Would you believe it? I hope so, because it's true. Being introverted - or extroverted for arguments sake - is all about how you process information and where you get your energy. One is no more a character flaw or handicap than the other. Put simply, introverts recharge their batteries by being alone while extroverts recharge theirs by socializing.

*"Introverts are like a rechargeable battery. They need to stop expending energy and rest in order to recharge. Extroverts are like solar panels that need the sun to recharge. Extroverts need to be out and about to refuel."*
~ Marti Olsen Laney

It is fair to say everybody has some key characteristics of introversion and extroversion. However, there is usually one side that is more dominant, which is what shapes who a person is in life. Knowing what makes you tic can help you make decisions about how to handle situations without conflicting with your inner extrovert or introvert personality. You don't have to force yourself into uncomfortable situations to prove you are a valuable member of society. You have plenty of strengths that will help make a difference.

In the text that follows, I will guide you from where you are to a place where you will be able to be true to yourself and let your introverted power shine through. I will also validate, vindicate, and enlighten you so you will be set-free to become the best possible version of who you were meant to be. You will find useful "how to" information covering everything from dating and networking to parties and public speaking - all the stuff of life that introverts usually have trouble with.

My goal for writing this book is so you will be able to accept who you are and know your strengths, so you can leverage them to your advantage in every situation. After all is said and done, being true to your own nature is the key to finding work you love and a life that matters. That is my hope and desire for you, so let's get started!

*"In a gentle way, you can shake the world."*
~ Gandhi

One last thing, as a way of saying Thank You for buying my book I have put together a **FREE GIFT** just for you!

**"Are You an Introvert?
A Short Quiz to Help You Find Out!"**

This gift is the perfect complement to this book so just head over to this web address to get the free download:

**https://tinyurl.com/2nm7c9bu**

# Chapter 1 - Introversion vs. Extroversion

The terms introversion and extroversion have been taken from the world of psychology and skewed a bit to fit into our world today. While the meanings are essentially the same, the word introvert is often used interchangeably with the word 'shy' to describe somebody who prefers staying at home instead of going out. The "sion" portion of the word makes it sound like either one is a condition of some sort that needs fixing. They aren't. The words are used by psychologists to identify how a person gathers strength and energy. This is an important distinction I want you to remember as you read this book. Perhaps the best way to think about it is introversion and extroversion are determined by where you feel the happiest and at peace with yourself.

When you compare the two, introversion and extroversion could be viewed as the negative and positive charge of a magnet. They are on opposite ends of a continuum. Carl Jung first identified the personality traits and the idea has expanded and evolved since its first use. The Myers-Briggs Type Indicator uses the theory to identify specific traits of a personality.

It is fair to say everybody has some key characteristics of introversion and extroversion. However, there is usually one side that is more dominant, which is what shapes who a person is in life. Jung explained that an extrovert may appreciate a quiet night in on occasion, but ideally, a night out is what really excites him.

Back in the mid 1,900's, Isabel Myers and her mother, Katherine Briggs studied Carl Jung's theories about personality. They reasoned learning how a person thought could lead to some pretty interesting information that could be applied in day to day life. In order to really fine tune the art of discovering if somebody was an introvert or an extrovert, they created a quick test. The test involves a person answering a series of questions. From there, the Myers-Briggs (personality) Type Indicator {MBTI} was put to work and voila, a person's personality 'type' was revealed.

It is important to point out that the MBTI isn't a test to discover some condition that needs to be treated or that would hold a person back from being happy or successful in life. In fact, it is really just the opposite. Knowing what makes you tick can help you make decisions about how to handle situations without conflicting with your inner extrovert or introvert personality.

## How introverts and extroverts think

What makes you tic? What makes your loud, outgoing friend tick? It is fun and rather important to establish just what determines our responses to certain outside influences. Knowing how we think can help us identify ways of coping, managing and even turning every situation into an opportunity.

According to Jung, introverts are internal thinkers. They need to spend some time analyzing and categorizing decisions and the outcomes of a decision. This isn't a process that can be done in a noisy, crowded room. The introvert would much rather absorb as much information as possible and then spend some time alone digesting it. Group sessions at work or even in the classroom are not ideal for an introvert.

An extrovert is just the opposite. An extrovert thrives when there is a lot of activity surrounding them and people are talking openly and tossing around ideas. The extrovert will be throwing out ideas as they come to him as well. An introvert is going to spend some time thinking before offering any suggestions or ideas. If an introvert is asked for an opinion, she will likely withhold it until she has fully processed it and decided exactly what her opinion is.

Introverts are prone to perfectionism while their extrovert counterparts are willing to "take the bull by the horns," so to speak, and accept whatever comes their way. The introvert's tendency towards perfection may require a little more time and energy, which means they will appreciate the quiet time to complete a project.

Here is another way to get inside the brain of an introvert and extrovert:

Imagine a brilliant flower. It needs plenty of sunshine, water and a healthy soil to survive. An introvert needs plenty of alone time, comfortable, familiar surroundings and a close friend or two to thrive. An extrovert needs lots of people around in a lively setting that spawns action and creativity.

The different environments are what give the introverts and extroverts their energy. They are polar opposites, but both very effective.

## Is Extroversion the Norm in Society?

It is true, the world caters to extroverts. Noise, bright lights and hives of activity are everywhere. Society has made it seem like those who shun public places are abnormal. How can anybody possibly enjoy their own company? If a person prefers spending time at home or at their best friend's house, they must be anti-social, because the "normal" way to be is out and about and whooping it up, so thinks the extrovert. It is abnormal to want to take time to think carefully about an idea or proposal before making a decision. Society has jumped in the fast lane and it isn't slowing down any time soon. The faster, the better seems to be the trend. Instead of choosing between a cheeseburger and a hamburger, there are 20 other sandwiches thrown into the mix these days.

Yes, the ideal personality trait in today's society leans towards extroversion. For an introvert, this can be a little difficult. Being on the speeding train with all the lights, noise, chatter and a hundred different options is sensory overload for an introvert. Oddly enough, about a third of the population is introverted. Doesn't it seem strange a fairly large percentage of society is ignored or shunned?

In the past, introverts may have struggled to get ahead in the world, but that is all changing. There are a lot more introverts out there than you would suspect, or society would even acknowledge. That is because introverts are not in your face, raising their hand declaring their introversion. They are at home or in their office quietly doing what they do best.

Introverts are typically born the way they are. From the moment they are born, children are encouraged to socialize and play with other children. They get into school and teachers are constantly telling them they need to play with other kids or work together on projects. Teachers will likely tell parents that their child is shy because he or she prefers to spend time in the library surrounded by books rather than out on the playground with the rest of the kids. Parents will follow the teacher's direction and tell their child no more reading at recess; they need to get out on the playground with the other kids and run around screaming and having a good time.

Inside, the child is withering. The noise and activity on the playground are too much and the child will likely show signs of further withdrawal in order to regroup. When the child gets home from school, spending time alone in his room isn't just something he wants to do, he NEEDS to do it. Unfortunately, it isn't understood, and the child will be labeled as antisocial, really quiet and withdrawn or shy.

When parents hear the child is withdrawn, society has taught us that something is wrong with the child. The child needs fixing and quick before she grows up like that.

Thankfully, those little scenarios are becoming fewer and further between (hopefully) as more introverts tell their stories. Introverts have found their voices and are expressing their thoughts and concerns, so others understand they are not shunning society, they simply need to be alone. It isn't anything personal. Everybody has their own wants and needs, and an introvert typically wants to be left alone.

# Chapter 2 - Are You an Introvert?

You may assume you are an introvert simply because you have been told a hundred times or more that you are really shy. Or maybe you have been referred to as anti-social. Well-meaning friends and family members may invite you to a party but then add something like, "Well we doubt you will come because you never like to leave the house," or something along those lines. You may feel like an introvert, but are you really?

If you haven't already, take the short quiz in the **FREE GIFT** offered with this book to find out if you're an introvert. It's fun, free, and only takes 2 minutes. Here's the link again:

**https://softpresspublishing.com/IntrovertQuiz**

If you have discovered you are not an introvert or maybe you already knew you were more of an extrovert, those situations may help you to understand what an introvert is thinking or feeling. You may realize that your introverted friend, co-worker or loved one isn't "different," but completely normal for their natural personality.

With that said, now that you know for sure you are an introvert, you can start rejoicing in your personality type and making it work for you. Throughout this book you are going to learn some tips and tricks for making your introvert personality a blessing instead of a curse, which is often what some make it out to be. How can it be wrong to appreciate your own company or to enjoy contemplating life?

## Strengths of the introvert

You are probably thinking, really? What could be so grand about being an introvert? Maybe you struggle to have fun at parties and your co-workers and acquaintances often make derogatory remarks about your lack of interest in their shenanigans. This can make it seem like being an introvert is a bad thing. You have probably even tried very hard to be more outgoing and to jump at the chance to hang out with a group of 100 strangers and pretended you enjoyed it.

You don't have to force yourself into uncomfortable situations to prove you are a valuable member of society. You have plenty of strengths that will help make a difference. Check them out below.

## Strong Leaders

Whether you realize it or not, your introversion is actually a desirable quality in a leader. Leaders, not dictators, are best when they can listen to those they are leading and acknowledge new ideas and visions. Introverts are more likely to be those quiet leaders who will sit in a board room listening to their managers and department heads toss around ideas, express their opinions and reveal their dreams for the company. The introverted leader is sitting quietly filing away all the bits and pieces of information to analyze later—alone in the office. Ideas that have merit are implemented and the masses will follow the quiet leader in the office upstairs. It is important an introverted leader is paired with the right team for the best chance of success. Many executives are able to match an introvert leader with the perfect team because they have seen it work in the past.

A few very successful leaders in business with introverted tendencies include Facebook founder Mark Zuckerberg, Former President Obama, Yahoo CEO Marissa Mayer and famed investor Warren Buffett.

## Good Friend

As an introvert, you tend to focus your time and energy on a couple of friends, rather than spreading yourself thin by trying to manage numerous relationships. Because you are more willing to invest in one or two people, you are a very good friend to have. Introverts are likely to prefer hanging out with their two best friends over hanging out with a group of friends at a loud bar or hopping dance club. You are able to form more solid relationships with your close friends by having conversations about things that truly matter. Your superior listening skills and ability to process information and provide advice based on deductive reasoning instead of emotion is appreciated. Your close friends will depend on you to be their rock, silent and steady, but always there.

## Really Good at a Specific Job/Hobby

Introverts like to really dig into something that appeals to them. They give it their all. Several hours a day might be devoted to thinking about a particular hobby or that report that is due in a week. All that time spent "inside your own head" is when the magic happens. If you love knitting, you would likely spend hours thinking about the task and all of the things you could make. You envision a pair of booties for your sister's new baby and how you will do each little chain to make it happen.

Introverts are not going to abandon a new hobby after a day or two and a huge investment of money just to discover they don't really like it. An introvert is going to spend some time thinking about the hobby and analyzing it before going out and buying a bunch of supplies. Introverts are willing to spend Friday night at home alone perfecting their hobby of choice. They don't care if they are missing out on a big dinner party with a large group of friends. The focus is on the hobby, which is what any talent or job needs in order to become really good at it. Introverts love perfectionism and will strive to reach it in everything they do.

## Overthinking is a Good Thing

You have probably been told a hundred times to stop trying to overthink everything. Well, doesn't that seem kind of silly? When you spend some quality time thinking about a project or an important decision, you are able to really identify all of the pros and cons. Making hasty decisions is for those who don't mind the consequences of shooting from the hip. An introvert will likely feel better about any choice they have made because they thought about it in depth and came to the decision after weighing all the options. They are less likely to experience harsh consequences from their choices. Every action has a reaction and the introvert is going to also contemplate that, which will be a learning experience. They will know better the next time and be able to make an even better choice.

## Self-Reliant

After a particularly stressful week at work, you may hear a co-worker asking people to go out for drinks on Friday night to unwind and recharge. You won't hear an introvert saying that. When that coworker can't find anybody available or willing to go out and kick up their heels, said coworker feels down. He *needs* to get out and mingle to recharge. An extrovert relies on the ability to be with other people to recharge, which isn't always a guaranteed option. An introvert just needs to go home and spend a quiet evening alone. He doesn't need to hang out with the guys and throw back a few beers while hooting and hollering at the television in an act of male bonding. Extroverted ladies may think a trip to the mall with five of their friends or a day at the spa with a dozen other women is the way to go. The introverts don't have to rely on others to help them recharge. They only have to count on themselves. They don't need to "get out" at all and would much rather stay in, alone.

## Shyness is not introversion

One of the biggest misconceptions about introversion is that introverts are just really shy. They just need to "come out of their shell" a little. Wrong! An introvert isn't always going to be shy per se. A person who isn't intent on being the center of attention everywhere he or she goes does not make them shy or anti-social. Many people assume an introvert who isn't talking much is too shy to do so. That isn't the case at all. The introvert is simply observing, assessing and contemplating whether or not they have anything of value to add to the conversation. If they don't, they are not going to speak up.

Unlike extroverts who like to talk and like to have everybody listening to what they say all the time, introverts only feel the need to speak when it is something worth saying. In fact, shy people would not be excited about giving a speech or presentation in front of a roomful of strangers, but an introvert may be perfectly okay with it. They would be fine with it because they were confident in what they had to present because they had spent a lot of time thinking and planning the presentation.

A shy person could do the same careful planning but be unable to stand in front of a group.

Author Sophia Dembling says it best when she references a neuroscientist who studies shyness. According to her, the scientist says, "Shyness is a behavior -– it's being fearful in a social situation. Whereas introversion is a motivation. It's how much you want and need to be in those interactions."[1]

Shyness is often something that can become so severe; it leads to severe anxiety and possibly even panic attacks when faced with a public situation. Anxiety can keep a person in their homes and stops them from enjoying life. Introversion is nothing like that. A shy person may long to be like others and feel as if they are missing out on life because they don't have the courage to talk to others. An introvert is totally cool with being alone. They thrive during their alone time. It makes them stronger.

---

[1] http://www.huffingtonpost.com/2013/07/29/introvert-myths_n_3569058.html

# Chapter 3 - Celebrating Introversion

Now that you know how awesome being an introvert really is, it is time to celebrate—alone most likely. There is no need to call up everybody you know (even if it is only 10 people) and invite them over to party. Rejoice in the fact you are a strong person who has a lot to offer the world. You don't have to feel as if you are an outcast or unworthy of success. You are completely normal. There isn't anything wrong with you and you don't need therapy to help you overcome your desire for peace and quiet.

It is time to shuck some of the labels you have been carrying around since your first day in kindergarten. Maybe your teachers and parents worried about you being a loner or worried you were too shy for your own good because you liked to read a book instead of chasing other kids around on the playground. This is a new world and people are coming to appreciate introverts and what they bring to the table, which is quite a bit. Isaac Newton, Bill Gates, and Albert Einstein were all introverts, and look at what they have done for the world. Their introspective nature that left them alone and with their own thoughts allowed them the time they needed to create some pretty awesome inventions and do amazing things. Your introversion can work in your favor, too.

## Introversion and Confidence

Many introverts struggle with self-confidence. Not because of anything they did, but typically because for the majority of their lives they have been told to be something different. That implies the person the introvert truly is, is wrong in some way. That can certainly knock down one's self-confidence. Being told you need to loosen up, get out more or you are anti-social makes it seem as though the things you enjoy and the way you are naturally, is wrong. For some, it can be a major blow to one's confidence. Fortunately, because of the way an introvert ticks, the things people say are not always taken to heart. Remember, an introvert gathers energy from being alone.

Deep down, introverts are not really lacking in confidence, but they appear that way because they are not spouting off everything they know from the rooftops. Introverts don't run around seeking out the praise of their peers and co-workers. They know what they know and that is all that really matters. Does that mean introverts lack self-confidence overall?

The confusion about confidence is all about perception. The introvert likely knows his stuff, but to somebody looking at him, he doesn't look confident. As we just discussed, introverts are often confused with being shy, when it isn't the case at all. Just because an introvert doesn't act like his extrovert counterpart, it doesn't mean there is a lack of confidence.

An introvert's body language may give off the impression of shyness or a lack of confidence. The introverted person isn't out there using wild hand gestures or speaking animatedly. The introvert is more of a "call it like they see it" kind of speaker. That may look like he doesn't have confidence, but really it is just the opposite. In an introvert's mind, why is there a need for all the smoke and mirrors when the facts are there? Flair and pizzazz are often wasted on an introvert.

## Talking to Extroverts

Talking with somebody who is a polar opposite can be tricky. You may stumble over what to say and the conversation may be stilted on your part. Your extrovert counterpart will likely do the majority of the talking, but as an active person in the conversation, you will be expected to make a comment here and there. In general, the notion of having a lengthy discussion with an extrovert is exhausting. It probably makes you cringe a bit and long for your couch and the four walls around it. It isn't that you don't like your extrovert friend or co-worker; it is more likely you don't know what to say or do because you are so different from each other.

Here are a few tips to help you feel better while talking with an extroverted friend, coworker or acquaintance and still do your part to foster a good relationship with them:

- Give the extrovert time to express opinions and to say whatever is on his mind. He really just wants somebody to listen and as an introvert, that is one of the things you do best. Don't be afraid to interrupt from time to time to ask a question. Don't stop talking altogether when the extrovert interrupts you while you speak—and it will happen.

- Compliment the extrovert in public. You can say you like their shoes, hair or purse or tell them they did a really good job on that project. Public praise is very appreciated by an extrovert.

- Try and make physical contact, whether it is a handshake, a hand on the shoulder or a hug. This is a big deal for most extroverts.

- Be prepared to offer your opinions. The extrovert values your opinions and will likely appreciate any suggestions you offer.

- When they are excited and animated, smile and encourage them. They will appreciate you accepting them and their vivid expressions and excitement. Sometimes, the really excitable extroverts may need to be taken in with small doses. You will probably not do well being around your vivacious friend 8 hours a day. Your energy will be depleted, and you will likely feel cranky and unwilling to tolerate much more from a friend you really like.

- If possible, surprise them from time to time. Show up at their office with their favorite Starbucks drink or accept one of their many invitations to grab lunch together.

**Using Introversion to Your Advantage**

Realize this: **Your introversion is one of your most important assets**. Your ability to listen and analyze is probably one of your greatest strengths and can help you in all areas of your life. You likely also have the memory of an elephant. Once a piece of information is processed through your brain, it is tucked away in a file and stored in a tidy little memory bank for future use.

Your long memory is a major advantage, but so is your ability to focus all of your time and energy on a particular task. When your boss gives you a job, he knows it is going to get done. You don't need him hanging over your shoulder asking you every five minutes how you are doing. At first, that may have been the case, but you have proven yourself time and again. You are dependable. This ability to focus and complete projects is something bosses look for. You will be climbing the career ladder in no time. What you don't say is made up for in your work. That is what bosses really look for. Lip service is only going to get somebody so far.

Think of your introversion as a panther. A panther is a silent, but powerful trait that is always there, just outside of view, waiting and watching for the right moment to strike. Take advantage of that quiet strength and be ready to apply it when necessary.

You don't have to be the loudest person in the room or the person who says the most. Your tendency to be quiet and observe has likely earned you respect. Your coworkers and friends know that when you do speak, it is something valuable and insightful. Learning how to choose your words carefully to express your opinion or observation will gain you a great deal of respect from those around you. You can use this to your advantage in all areas of life. Your spouse, kids, coworkers and friends have come to love you for who you are, and they know when you say something, it is important. They will stop, and they will listen, which is a very big deal in this day and age when meaningless information is spewed out at rapid rates.

# Chapter 4 - Socialization for Introverts

Blech! Socialization, do you really have to? Yes, you do, but it doesn't have to be all that bad. In fact, many introverts enjoy socializing from time to time. The difference between an introvert and extrovert is the frequency and duration of the desire for hanging out with others. An introvert may enjoy a quiet dinner party with close friends for a couple of hours once a month or maybe once every couple of weeks.

Many people assume socialization has to involve clubbing or attending functions where hundreds of people are milling about making small talk. That is not something an introvert will ever enjoy. It is possible to be an introvert and enjoy some socialization and even dating!

**Networking**

In the business world, you need to be able to network in order to make contacts and keep your bosses happy and do a good job. If you are one of the bosses (which is very possible for an introvert) then you know you need to network in order to stay abreast of current events related to your particular area of business. This can be a bit exhausting for an introvert if you have to network all day long!

Here are some helpful tips to get you through any networking event:

- Plan your networking events to give you plenty of time to reenergize. If you are planning on attending a function that will be all about networking, give yourself 30 minutes alone before you are scheduled to be there. Network for a bit and then step outside under the guise of taking a phone call and just give yourself 5 to 10 minutes to regroup.

- Practice a few questions that you can ask a new contact. Come up with a few open ended questions that will get the other person talking and will take some of the pressure off of you. While the standard, "Boy this weather...." is certainly an okay conversation starter, you will be expected to continue the flow of small talk. Ask things like, "How long have you been with your company?" or "What made you decide to get into this line of work?"

- Quality conversations during networking events are much more productive than running around the room talking to every single person. If you have struck up an interesting conversation that provides you with helpful information, continue it. Don't feel pressured to cut it short in order to move on to the next person.

- It isn't a race to collect the most email addresses, phone numbers or other social-networking names. Having 500 people follow you on Twitter doesn't mean a thing if they don't know who you are, what you do and what appeals to you. If you are not interested in sending somebody emails or having them send you emails, don't volunteer the information or ask for theirs. Finally, keep in mind that one genuine, new relationship is worth a shoebox full of business cards.

## Public Speaking

It is completely natural to feel a little apprehension when it comes to speaking in front of a group. Most people experience this whether they are extroverts or introverts. You can make the task of public speaking a little more manageable by following these tips:

- Enjoy a few moments of peace and quiet before you need to deliver your speech. Do some deep breathing exercises to calm your nerves. Review your notes and give yourself a little pep talk. You can do this because you know what you are talking about.

- While you are up at the podium, smile. Give a huge smile whether you are feeling it or not. The simple act of smiling helps give you a burst of confidence while setting your nerves at ease. Your audience will also feel like you are happy to be there and will likely smile back. A smiling audience is always much easier to talk to than an audience filled with stone-faced people.

- Imagine yourself as a performer. Your job is to deliver a speech. You are not that person. You are simply acting out a part. This can help you step out of who you are and be somebody else who is comfortable doing public speaking.

- Know your material forwards and backwards. As an introvert, you are probably pretty familiar with whatever it is you are going to be speaking on. This alone gives you confidence. You know what you are talking about and you know you can impart a great deal of knowledge to your listeners. Thrive on that confidence and deliver your information like you were talking to your best friend. Just be you!

## Dating for Introverts

Dating can be a scary thought for anybody! The idea of meeting new people and picking their brains and trying to discover if there is even a hint of romantic feelings can be exhausting. Trying to get to know somebody and investing a lot of time and energy into the process only to discover they are not right for you is taxing, but it is one of those things that must be done. As an introvert, all the socializing to find that perfect mate is a little overwhelming.

These tips can help you make it through the dating world and will hopefully lead you to your future lifelong mate:

- Use your natural listening skills to your advantage. This will help you quickly identify things you like or possibly don't like about a particular person. By allowing somebody to talk, you can learn a lot about who they are. Create some open-ended questions that will help you discover who a person really is deep down. An avid listener (that's you) is a beautiful quality in a potential match.

- Choose places to meet at that will not make you nervous or uncomfortable. Loud, crowded bars are not typically an introvert's cup of tea. Ask to meet at a park where you can take advantage of a quiet space on a park bench or in a restaurant that gives you the privacy and calm environment you need to have a quality conversation with somebody.

- If you are struggling to meet people, try visiting places where you are likely to find like-minded singles. A museum, zoo, coffeehouse, church, volunteering or even night classes at the community college are all great places to meet others who share your interests. Don't be afraid to try online dating as well. You'll have the ability to review potential matches from the comfort of your own home.

- Be yourself from the very beginning. You may feel like you should love hanging out at a club because your date does or that you should love visiting art museums and going gaga over an abstract piece of art. Don't do it. You need to let that person know from the get go that clubbing isn't your cup of tea. They will get it or they won't.

- Do NOT rely on 'liquid courage' (aka: alcohol) to make you open up and transform into an extrovert. That is a recipe for disaster. A little drink here or there is okay, but don't get so drunk you become somebody you are not. Eventually and hopefully, you will meet the person when you are sober, and you will be exactly who you are without the false pretenses.

- Don't be afraid to tell your date that you do not particularly like certain things. It is best to get all the information out before you invest time, energy and your heart into a relationship that will never go anywhere. It is up to the other person to decide if they like what they see.

## Party Survival Skills

Ack! A party! Hours of watching other people laugh and have a good time while you hug the wall and count down the minutes until it is over. Introverts by nature are not big party animals. It is a seemingly unnecessary ritual that holds no appeal for a person who gathers their energy from being alone or in small groups of close friends. You can still mingle at parties and get that socialization that extroverts are convinced you need. And, you can even enjoy yourself! Here are some tips for doing just that:

- Ask a close friend, who you are comfortable with, to attend the party with you. Let your friend do the socializing and ice breaking and ease you into a conversation. This gives you moral support and an anchor.

- Arrive early enough that you can leave early without offending the host. Typically, 2 hours is considered socially acceptable to hang out at a party. By arriving early, you are doing your part to show up before the party really starts rocking and rolling.

- Take a few breaks from the activity to reenergize. Either step outside and sit on the patio for a few minutes or go the bathroom and gather your wits. A few deep breaths in a quiet place can restore your resolve to stick it out for another 30 minutes.

- Try out some small talk while you are at home looking in the mirror. The more familiar you become with saying the words, the easier it is to say them to a stranger. Don't be afraid of the standard, "How are you liking this weather?" line. It works and is an excellent ice breaker.

- Do not reach for your phone and use it as your best friend at the party. Candy Crush or solitaire can wait. If you have your face glued to your phone all night, you are going to miss the opportunity to meet others, even if it is only a couple of people.

# Chapter 5 - Fearing Solitude vs. Courage to Be Alone

Sometimes, feelings get a little mixed up. The signals that are hitting the brain can become crossed and it can be difficult to determine what you really feel. Extroverts tend to fear solitude and often admire an introvert's courage to be alone. However, it is totally natural for an introvert to thrive in their own company. In fact, what they typically fear most is being immersed in public all the time.

There is something to be said for solitude, but it can be a bit scary. Even an introvert can fear being truly alone in life. While they appreciate their own company, human nature is to have a close companion or two. Introverts often struggle with those opposing forces. On one hand, you want to be closed up at home reading a book and content with your own thoughts. On the other hand, you may fear your desire for being alone may end up making you a loner for the rest of your life.

Sometimes, it can take real courage to be alone and at peace with oneself. Spending that time alone is what makes an introvert truly blossom. You will have time to reflect on what you want and make plans on how to get it. If that means you want to be married and have a gaggle of children, you can set goals and gather up the courage to start dating.

Learning to appreciate one's own company is a powerful thing. It gives a person a great deal of inner strength because they know exactly who they are. They don't need another person to tell them how fabulous they are, although a meaningful compliment would never be discouraged.

There are plenty of quotes that praise solitude. One favorite has to do with the person who walks with a crowd will only go as far as the crowd. The person who isn't afraid to be alone will go farther than the crowd. Albert Einstein, who was a notorious introvert, came up with that observation.

Face it, we live in an extroverted society. Introverts often feel like they have to conform in order to be like the rest of the crowd. You don't! You don't have to be afraid of being different from the rest of your co-workers, friends or family. If you are okay being alone, so be it. It comes down to what makes you happiest in life. Your time alone in reflection is critical to your overall happiness. You need that time to sort everything out. Introverts do not have to fear the solitude they crave. Embrace it. Own it and make it work for you.

**Paralysis by Analysis**

Sometimes, introversion can leave you stuck in the mud. You spend so much time analyzing and contemplating a task or decision, you ultimately paralyze yourself. You can't move forward because you are so stuck in the process of analyzing every possible outcome. Have you ever just felt so overwhelmed by all the different options on a restaurant menu you just kind of freeze up? It is like an assault to your brain. You can't possibly spend 4 hours looking at each dish and deciding which one would be the most satisfying, the most economical or the best dish for your diet. You get that frozen, deer-in-the-headlights look when faced with too many options. Your introverted brain cannot possibly make a spontaneous decision—or can it?

Some of your hesitation to make a decision may be due to the fear of making a wrong decision. Introverts are careful decision makers. It is part of what makes them tick. They need that quiet reflection to analyze options based on information they have collected. When there isn't enough time or information, the introvert may freeze up a bit or become paralyzed.

An introvert who experiences 'paralysis by analysis' will often rely on a good friend or their spouse to make the decision for them. This fixes the immediate problem of giving an order or choosing a color of paint for the wall while standing in line at the home improvement store, but these kinds of decisions are likely to leave an introvert feeling a little out of sorts.

So, how can you avoid that sickening feeling & situation? These tips will help you avoid the crippling paralysis introverts are known to suffer from when faced with too many options:

- Set clear deadlines. If you have a lot of data to categorize or information to collect, give yourself a time frame. You will collect as much information as possible in 24 hours or 1 week, whatever the case may be. If you have to make a decision about something, give yourself 24 hours, a week or 2 minutes. You don't want to extend your agony any longer than necessary and contemplating a decision can be extremely stressful.

- Determine whether or not the decision you are faced with is really worth your complete concentration. Will your choice affect you a year from now or change the course of your life in some way? If we are talking about choosing what to eat at a restaurant--probably not. If you are choosing what job offer to accept, yes, it most definitely deserves your attention.

- Understand that perfection is not usually going to be attainable. Most often, "close enough" is really all you need. This can be a tough one for introverts who like to spend a lot of time and energy plotting the perfect move. Not every decision is going to have perfect results. Don't let it stress you out or sway you. Embrace the little imperfections and use them to your advantage the next time you are faced with a similar situation. Experience and mistakes are what make you wise. You will know the results of a particular choice and can quickly eliminate the option from your array of options in the future.

- Define what your ultimate goal is. Is it to eat healthy, choose a job that has career advancement opportunities or choose a color of paint that will match your furniture? Outlining what it is you hope to achieve will help you make decisions to reach that goal.

- Ask a trusted friend or your spouse for their opinion. You want to have formed your own idea before asking. So something like, "Do you think I should go with the grilled fish or the spaghetti?" You have narrowed the menu down to two items and are simply asking for a little help making that important, final decision.

- Rely on your gut instinct. Typically, those first, immediate decisions or inclinations towards a particular choice are the best. Our natural instinct is usually the best option for us. The paralysis comes in and makes that easy choice a murky one and you are thrust into an uncertain area where you must evaluate each and every option.

- Use the process of elimination. Automatically eliminate choices you know right away are not right for you and are not going to help you reach your goal. If it is a particular color, a particular food or a job that doesn't appeal to you at all, don't waste your time thinking twice about it. Eliminating 10 items and leaving yourself with only 5 to contemplate is a huge help and can make the process of making a decision much easier.

Introverts are especially prone to paralysis by analysis. It is often one of the traits that introverts do not like about themselves. However, it is also one of their best attributes. Being able to make thoughtful, careful decisions is not a bad thing. Yes, it can become a little overwhelming and may frustrate your extroverted friends who are willing to take risks without thinking about the consequences, but it is also why they like you. You are likely their solid footing and can help reel them in when necessary. Split second decision making is not for everybody. When a choice deserves your full attention, give it your all. Don't get too caught up in the hundreds of little decisions you will be faced with every day.

# Chapter 6 - Managing Self-Doubt

Introverts often get so caught up in thinking about every aspect of their lives they start to doubt what they have and what choices they have made. They begin to question their abilities and can really work up a very strong case of self-doubt about almost anything. A lot of the uncertainty is spurred by the desire to make perfect choices based on careful consideration of all the information gathered.

Introverts are natural perfectionists. Wait for it---**nobody is perfect!** Unfortunately, that is a concept introverts tend to understand, but try to reach it anyway. Much of the critical thoughts an introvert comes up with about their own life is due to all that time alone thinking about things. Extroverts don't often have to worry about doubting themselves because they don't like to spend a lot of time doing a lot of self-analyzing. They are more of a fly-by-the-seat-of-their-pants type and rarely allow self-doubt to creep in. While that might make introverts a little envious of their counterparts, you too can help manage those critical thoughts that creep up from time to time.

First, let's talk about how to identify self-doubt. Typically, there are going to be some phrases you use while you are talking to your friend or thinking in your own head:

- Maybe, I shouldn't or maybe I should have done this;

- This is probably too difficult;

- I am not sure if this is right, I think I am wrong;

- Maybe this isn't right for me.

When those things start to enter your mind, or you hear yourself saying them to somebody else, it is time to stop and do what you can to quiet the doubts that are threatening to derail you and keep you from doing what you know you can. Now, those little phrases mentioned above are not always going to lead you down a terrible path. However, they are your first inclination that you are not completely comfortable with something. Consider them your warning bells. Sometimes you need to pay attention and other times it is a false alarm.

If you begin to get that uncomfortable, slightly jittery feeling about a particular task you are doing or a decision you have made, quickly take the following action to try and quiet the self-doubt:

- Apply your critical thinking to disprove a particular thought of self-doubt. If you need to, write it down. Write down all the reasons the insecurity isn't true. Sometimes, you just need a little reaffirming that you have done the right thing or are doing your absolute best.

- Try to determine where the doubt is coming from. Is it because you have done a similar job before and it didn't go quite as planned? Maybe the doubt stems from personal insecurities and completing a task is the one way to abolish those insecurities. When you know where the doubt stems from, you can work at that one particular area.

- Use those introverted analyzing skills to create an action plan. It helps to have a clear path outlined. If you have a 20 page report due on Friday, create an action plan that will help you reach your goal. Monday you will do the outline, Tuesday you will do research, Wednesday you will write the report, Thursday you will review it and Friday—it's done!

- If you can find no logical reason for the doubt, but it is still there lingering in the back of your mind, try a little positive self-talk. "I know I can do this," "I am making the right decision," "I have done my best and I am happy with the results," are all examples of positive affirmation you could use to combat those negative thoughts that are threatening to derail you. Talk with a friend about what you are feeling. Your friend will likely be able to tell you the doubts are not valid. Sometimes a little praise and cheerleading is just what you need.

Not all doubt is a bad thing. If you are doubting yourself, there may be a valid reason for it. Sometimes, your subconscious knows more than your waking, conscious mind and it needs to be listened to. By analyzing your doubt, you are giving it the attention it deserves and determining whether it is warranted. In some cases, your doubt could be turned into a learning experience. You don't want to make the same mistake twice.

## Depression

Introverts are at a higher risk of suffering from depression than their extroverted counterparts. It is a serious condition that deserves adequate attention by not only the introvert, but their loved ones. A study[2] done back in 2002 revealed about 74 percent of introverts suffered from some type of depression. According to study author, David Janowsky MD, "Increased introversion predicts the persistence of depressive symptoms and a lack of remission."

One of the reasons the introvert is more susceptible to depression is the likelihood there are very few people who are allowed in the introvert's inner circle. Without others being able to identify the signs and symptoms of depression, it can go unchecked.

For the introvert, the signs may go unnoticed because they are so used to being closed off and actually enjoy being alone with their thoughts. It isn't always easy to recognize when the solitude is becoming too much. You can have too much of a good thing.

The following are some signs you may be suffering from depression and not just being the typical introvert. They can be difficult to distinguish because of an introvert's natural inclination to exhibit some of these signs.

- More withdrawn from public than usual.

- Lack of appetite or excessive appetite—any changes are a sign.

- Sleep habits change, either sleeping more or less than normal.

- Lack of energy or motivation to do much of anything.

---

[2] http://www.sciencedirect.com/science/article/pii/S0022395601000437

- Low self-esteem, excessive criticism of oneself.

- Feeling helpless, as if there is no other way out of the rut you have fallen into.

If you feel you are experiencing depression when you identify with any of these symptoms, it is important you take immediate action. Seek out a qualified medical professional immediately! You don't want the depression to consume you.

- First, you must identify the counterfeit feelings that have snuck in and are bringing you down. Do the feelings have any basis or is it simply your mind playing tricks on you? For example: are your depressing thoughts based on an assumption of what somebody else thinks or a prediction about an outcome of a particular project? These are not actual realities and it is up to you to sort through the feelings and thoughts that stem from this perceived concept. It can be a bit tough, but introverts are experts at analyzing and will be able to pinpoint the problem with a little self-examination.

- When you recognize the symptoms, give yourself a little break. Don't take on a big project or force yourself to go to a party because your friend says you need to get out. Introverts don't get their energy like that. While you will need some socialization, draining your energy by attending a party or hitting the clubs could send you deeper into depression.

- Do not be afraid to seek out the services of a professional counselor or therapist. The one-on-one setting is ideal for an introvert. While there may be some trust issues at first, counselors are trained to listen and are going to be familiar with introverts that are struggling to open up to a stranger. Group therapy is probably not your best option as an introvert. If you are already depressed, you don't need to tax yourself by putting yourself in an uncomfortable, emotionally draining situation. There is also the chance you will be so busy listening and analyzing other group members, your own concerns will be ignored.

- Pat yourself on the back for completing a task. If you have felt like you are stuck in a rut or simply don't have the motivation to do much of anything, set a goal to complete a rather easy task and then celebrate the completion. If that is to clean up the kitchen or do some gardening, make sure you reward yourself after it is done. It is like getting a little dose of happiness one spoonful at a time. You have to start small and slowly climb up and out of your depression. There isn't a switch you can flip to turn it off. You can't "snap out of it" like so many people are likely to tell you.

- Sitting at home is okay, it is how you recharge, but you don't want to sit at home with the blinds closed, the ringer off and the lights off. If you know you tend to have feelings that can make you depressed, dispel them with light! Create a relaxing, yet energizing atmosphere. Leave the blinds open or turn on a cheery light. Put on some music (not depressing music) and light a scented candle. You need to recharge, but you don't want to get mired in the muck, so to speak by feeding the depression.

- Give yourself time to do something you have been wanting to but have always said you didn't have the time.

34

If that is watching reruns of your favorite TV show or movie with a bowl of popcorn and a soda, go for it. You need something to distract you a bit from those depressing thoughts. Being in your comfort zone will make it easier for you to relax and enjoy yourself. Read a book, play your favorite computer game or whatever it is that you really enjoy that will not leave your brain idle and left to dwell on negative things.

Feeling depressed from time to time is normal. The problem introverts have is the feelings can be consuming because of the natural desire to sit and stew on a particular matter in an attempt to analyze it. It is a lot like a snowball rolling downhill. The more you think about the problem and close yourself off from your friends and family, the further you are falling into depression. Your loved ones know you and are used to you shutting yourself off and don't realize what is happening until the depression has really taken hold.

Do your best to take care of yourself. Take time to pamper yourself from time to time and give yourself a break.

# Conclusion

You've no doubt noticed that society has made a drastic shift from valuing the person you are to who you portray. It's no secret that individuals are frequently rewarded for personality over merit and the vocally dominant tend to win out over those who are, perhaps, more well-informed. Throughout this book I have given you many tips and tricks for making your introvert personality a blessing instead of a curse.

I trust you now understand and fully believe that being introverted has much more to do with how you process information and where you get your energy than any sort of character flaw or handicap. And, now that you know what makes you tic, you are better equipped to make decisions and deal with uncomfortable situations without conflicting with your inner personality.

We've discussed many of the things that cause introverts discomfort – parties, networking events, dating, and even public speaking – and I've given you tons of useful information and valuable tips for navigating these affairs, so you can leverage your inner power and strengths and use them to your best advantage. Never again compromise yourself, but instead, be true to who you are and love the life you live, for it is the only one you have.

# CONCLUSION

Finally, if you enjoyed this book, please take the time to share your thoughts and post a positive review on Amazon. I would greatly appreciate it!

**PS:** Self-confidence is something we all need, but unfortunately, we can't just run out to the store and buy it. It is something that must come from within, and for some, it can be incredibly difficult to achieve. If your self-esteem is taking a whipping or you are spinning your wheels trying to achieve your goals, my book "**Self Confidence Secrets: *Quickly and Easily Boost Your Self Esteem and Confidence Today so You Can Start to Achieve Anything, Make More Money, and Live the Life You've Always Wanted.***" contains the proven steps and strategies you need to increase your self-confidence quickly.

I will show you how to change your life for the better and boost your self-esteem in the process using simple, easy-to-learn skills and exercises that will give you a lifetime full of meaning and happiness. **Get it on Amazon Kindle today!**

# References

http://www.myersbriggs.org/my-mbti-personality-type/mbti-basics/extroversion-or-introversion.asp

http://www.huffingtonpost.com/2013/08/20/introverts-signs-am-i-introverted_n_3721431.html

http://psychology.about.com/od/psychologicaltesting/a/myers-briggs-type-indicator.htm

http://psychology.about.com/od/trait-theories-personality/f/introversion.htm

http://www.psychologytoday.com/blog/evil-deeds/201205/essential-secrets-psychotherapy-jungs-typology-eudaemonology-and-the-elusive-

http://www.psychologytoday.com/blog/fulfillment-any-age/201403/nine-signs-you-re-really-introvert

http://elitedaily.com/life/15-signs-you-are-an-introvert-and-are-secretly-obsessed-with-it/

https://www.americanexpress.com/us/small-business/openforum/articles/quiet-influence-6-advantages-introvert/

http://www.forbes.com/sites/bonniemarcus/2013/10/28/leaning-back-the-power-of-introverts/

http://psychcentral.com/lib/the-benefits-of-being-an-introvert/0001060/2

http://www.the-inner-net.com/introvert-weaknesses/

http://knowledgenuts.com/2014/03/07/the-difference-between-being-shy-and-being-introverted/

http://www.quietlyfabulous.com/2013/10/14/confidence-looks-different-for-introverts/

http://blog.bufferapp.com/introverts-and-extroverts-what-they-are-and-how-to-get-along-with-everyone

http://www.thegrindstone.com/2012/02/06/career-management/how-to-make-introversion-work-to-your-advantage-604/

http://www.huffingtonpost.com/diane-gottsman/networking-tips-for-intro_b_4978786.html

http://www.duarte.com/blog/public-speaking-for-introverts-6-essential-tips/

http://www.psychologytoday.com/blog/quiet-the-power-introverts/201107/10-public-speaking-tips-introverts

http://www.jordangrayconsulting.com/2013/02/introverts-guide-to-dating/

http://psychcentral.com/blog/archives/2012/04/16/5-quick-dating-tips-for-introverts/

http://www.doctornerdlove.com/2012/09/dating-introverts/all/1/

http://www.inc.com/ilan-mochari/4-tips-holiday-parties.html

http://www.purposefairy.com/6696/have-the-courage-to-walk-alone/

http://www.scientificamerican.com/article/the-power-of-introverts/

http://personalexcellence.co/blog/analysis-paralysis/

http://www.reliableplant.com/Read/18128/analysis-paralysis

http://advancedlifeskills.com/blog/7-simple-steps-to-conquering-self-doubt/

http://zenhabits.net/conquer-self-doubt/

http://www.ipersonic.com/blog_files/Introverted-and-happy-in-your-Job.html

http://www.healthcentral.com/depression/c/84292/115984/personalities/

http://afeatheroftruth.wordpress.com/2013/04/15/tips-for-a-depressed-introvert/

http://www.theguardian.com/technology/2012/apr/01/susan
-cain-extrovert-introvert-interview

http://greatist.com/happiness/why-society-should-support-
introverts-highly-sensitive-people

www.ingramcontent.com/pod-product-compliance
Lightning Source LLC
Chambersburg PA
CBHW071342310526
45790CB00018B/1062